SPEAKS LOUDER

21 Days of Love

Love

SPEAKS LOUDER

21 Days of Love

by
David Shannon Wooten

LOVE SPEAKS LOUDER
21 Days of Love

All Scripture quotations, unless otherwise indicated, are taken from
the Holy Bible, New International Version®, NIV®. Copyright
©1973, 1978, 1984, 2011 by Biblica, Inc.™ Used by permission of
Zondervan. All rights reserved worldwide.

First Edition: April 2018
Printed in the United States of America
ISBN: 978-0-692-09881-3

Cover Design: Amanda Wipperman
Interior Layout: David Shannon Wooten

To My Wife, Children & Newspring Church

I dedicate this book to my wife, Bonnie, who has loved me unconditionally. She has demonstrated to me throughout our 25 years of marriage and ministry what God's love looks like in action. I want to thank her for help in writing this book.

I dedicate this book to my children, Shantelle, Shalene and Ross, who have taught me more about love than any seminar or seminary ever could. My children have truly helped me to understand how to give and to demonstrate love better.

I dedicate this book to my Newspring Church family. It is a joy to give love in action to a church family who loves in return. Every week, I witness their love to others within our congregation and to the people in our community. Thank you for being a student and an example of God's love.

.

Introduction

Go anywhere in the world, and you will find variations of two universal behaviors. Actions inspired by love, and an extreme dichotomy of hatred. When we are intentional about love we prepare ourselves to rise to be the very best that God created us to be. Actions of love will drive out darkness. These intentional behaviors of love have the potential to change relationships, home environments, hearts children, corporate culture, church and our own community.

To know love in its purest form, we must go to the origin. We must learn from our Heavenly Father, who is Love. "Whoever does not love does not know God, because God is love" (1 John 4:8).

We can determine the type of tree by glancing at the fruit it is bearing. But if we really want to know the longevity of that tree's health, we must also inspect the root system and core. Similarly, when the love of Christ is in our core, everything will be in order and will produce the right result in our life. Dig all the way down and inspect the motivation of the action, behavior or thought. Love inspires us to give, to forgive, to show mercy, to help, to give our time, to listen, and to pray. When our actions are motivated by the love of Christ in our heart, they will produce incredible results.

My passion is to share the message of Love Speaks Louder. I pray that you will use this devotional book to spark your day with a Scripture and thoughts that give context to God's principles of love. Taking the time to reflect on what the Holy Spirit is speaking to your heart will, in turn, increase your level and impact of love.

Ⓦdavidshannonwooten.com

We all need to be on the receiving end of love. God has promised us that we will receive when we follow His principle. "Give, and it will be given to you. A good measure, pressed down, shaken together and running over, will be poured into your lap. For with the measure you use, it will be measured to you" (Luke 6:38). His principle is always to give first, and then to receive. Sow the seed; receive a harvest. You may not have the desired outcome today, but rather than focus on what you are currently receiving, instead nurture a foundation of giving. Sow seeds of Christ's love today and you will rejoice in your harvest tomorrow.

Love is the foundation for everything good in life. Be Christ's love. I pray the next 21 days you will experience a revival of love. And that the people you come in contact with will experience Christ's love through you.

Day 1
Redefining Love

"Dear friends, let us love one another, for love comes from God. Everyone who loves has been born of God and knows God. Whoever does not love does not know God, because God is love. This is how God showed his love among us: He sent his one and only Son into the world that we might live through him" (1 John 4:7-9).

Songs demonstrate how our culture views love. Do you remember some of these song titles: "When a man loves a woman," "Can't help falling in love," "Crazy in love," "Power of love," "I want to know what love is," "You make loving fun," "Is this love," and my all-time favorite (sarcasm) that makes no sense at all - "If loving you is wrong, I don't want to be right."

What?

DEFINING LOVE.

Our culture defines love in a totally different than the way in which God defines love. The American Heritage Dictionary defines love as "A strong feeling of affection and concern toward another person, as that arising from kinship or close friendship."[1] Most of the time, when a person is expressing their definition of love, it is based on conditions, feelings or emotions. But that is not God's definition of love. His love is unconditional. His love for us is not based on what we do for Him, but rather what He gave to us. God loves us not because we make Him feel good. God is the very definition of love. God loves; therefore, He gives (John 3:16). God gave His best gift,

1

His Son Jesus Christ, before we decided to love Him back (Romans 5:8).

> How we love will determine how we know
> God.

KNOW GOD, KNOW LOVE.

The more we develop our relationship with God and understand how He loves, the more we will be able to redefine how we love others. God has a standard of how we should love. This is the standard that determines how well we know God. "Everyone who loves, is born of God and knows God."

REFLECT:

- What is God revealing about Himself through this scripture?

- In what areas do you need to redefine love?

- How can you demonstrate unconditional love today, with the people in your life?

Day 2
First Love

"We love because he FIRST loved us" (1 John 4:19).

We didn't love God first. We are FIRST loved by God. Our first step towards knowing true love is to allow God to love us. We receive His love by accepting His "love gift," which is Jesus Christ, His Son. Any other effort to fill our hearts will fall short.

A paraphrased quote from one of Blaise Pascal's writings illustrates the point: **"There is a God-shaped vacuum in the heart of every person, and it can never be filled by any created thing. It can only be filled by God, made known through Jesus Christ."**[2]

When our relationship with God is strong, we feel more confident in His love for us. The **more** that we rely on God's love, we are **less** likely to feel insecure about ourselves. **This is SO important, not because we need to feel better about ourselves, but because we need to be free to show other people the love that God has given to us.**

Ravi Zacharias said, **"The love of God shows us that God alone bridges the distance between him and us, enabling us to see this world through Calvary."**[3] When we are confident in God's love toward us, we can see the people in our lives as God sees them. God wants us to see the people in our lives through the eyes of His own love.

LOVING GOD FIRST.

- **How we love others will demonstrate how we love God.** (1 John 4:20)

- **Loving God first will eliminate insecurities, jealousy or other selfish feelings that inhibit us from showing God's love.**

You will be free to give compliments, to celebrate others on their successes, to show kindness to people who are rude to you, to always speak well of people, and to never repeat someone's weakness to others.

When you love God first you will love others best.

God will fill you with His love. This will allow you to love people from His love in you. You cannot give people that which you do not possess.

Your spouse, your children, your friends, your students, your team, your coworkers, and your community need you to place a priority on loving God first.

We can help people find God's love through our acts of love. **First love God and BE the love to others.**

REFLECT:

- What is God revealing about Himself through this scripture?

- What actions, habits or behaviors demonstrate that you have placed a priority on loving God first?

- How are you able to love better as you place a priority on loving God first?

Day 3
This Is Unstoppable Love

"But God showed his great love for us by sending Christ to die for us while we were still sinners" (Romans 5:8).

The purest form of giving out of love is giving without the expectation of anything in return. Giving when it's not deserved. Giving something that really means a lot to you. I'm sure you have given under similar circumstances. You gave something, simply because you loved. Have you ever withheld giving, because you didn't think the person would appreciate it? I'll be honest – I have refrained from giving for that exact reason.

THE REAL DEFINITION AND STANDARD FOR LOVE.

God wants us to experience forgiveness and eternal life. He goes beyond telling us He loves us. He "showed" His love by giving us His Son, Jesus. This is the kind of GREAT love that God is demonstrating to you...

1. **God gave "while we were still sinners."** He gave you Jesus when you were not worthy.

2. **God gave without expecting anything in return.** He didn't wait until He knew for sure you would appreciate and receive Jesus.

3. **God gave His most valuable gift to you.** He gave his one and only Son, Jesus.

God has defined and set the standard for the purest form of love. This is the level of love that is unstoppable in its power to transform the individual heart and humanity. This kind of love spreads like wild fire that can cover families, communities, cities and countries.

When God's love is accepted and received, Christ comes in to our hearts and begins to reset the definition and standard of love in our own life. Because of Christ within us, we are able to give love like God loves.

WHAT IF EVERYONE GAVE LOVE…

- **… whether people were worthy of our love or not?**

- **… even if people did not appreciate or accept our demonstration of love?**

- **… sacrificially? Gifts that mean something to us.**

Unstoppable love began with God. His desire is to see His kind of love cover the entire world. This is the whole point of God sending His Son. He loved the world and wants to reach all of humanity with His love. This will only happen as we demonstrate the love that has been given to us.

We will be able to love at a higher level when we truly are confident of how God loves us.

REFLECT:

- What is God revealing about Himself through this scripture?

- How has God's love had a continued and ongoing effect on your life?

- What act of love can you do today that will lead people towards Christ's love?

Day 4
Love Is Committed

"And I am certain that God, who began the good work within you, will continue his work until it is finally finished on the day when Christ Jesus returns" (Philippians 1:6).

GOD WILL NEVER WALK OUT ON YOU.

God will never turn His back on you. He has begun a work in your heart and He is committed to following it through to completion. He created you for something amazing. Setbacks, rejection and a season of loss do not have the final say over God's plan for your life.

> Any thought that brings doubt to your self-worth is not from your Heavenly Father.

God's love for you is not fickle. He proved His love and commitment to you when He gave you His ultimate "Gift of Love," EVERLASTING life through His Son, Jesus. His love was unwavering then, just as it remains firm today. And it will be consistent for your entire life.

YOUR FATHER IS COMMITTED TO FINISHING WHAT HE HAS STARTED IN YOU.

Be patient. You may feel that you are not making progress, but you cannot see every detail that God sees. Remember, God knows the entire plan for your life because He created it.

Since God's love is consistent and committed to you, keep your trust consistent and committed to Him. Your Father is a Creator, a Designer, an Architect, and an Artist. Enjoy the amazing work that God is creating in you.

REFLECT:

- What is God saying to you through this Scripture?

- When and where are you tempted to not be committed?

- God is committed to you. How will you remain committed to God's plan for your life?

Day 5
Love Brings Victory

"What, then, shall we say in response to these things? If God is for us, who can be against us? He who did not spare his own Son, but gave him up for us all—how will he not also, along with him, graciously give us all things? Who will bring any charge against those whom God has chosen? It is God who justifies. Who then is the one who condemns? No one. Christ Jesus who died—more than that, who was raised to life—is at the right hand of God and is also interceding for us. Who shall separate us from the love of Christ? Shall trouble or hardship or persecution or famine or nakedness or danger or sword? As it is written: 'For your sake we face death all day long; we are considered as sheep to be slaughtered.' No, in all these things we are more than conquerors through him who loved us. For I am convinced that neither death nor life, neither angels nor demons, neither the present nor the future, nor any powers, neither height nor depth, nor anything else in all creation, will be able to separate us from the love of God that is in Christ Jesus our Lord" (Romans 8:31-39).

NOTHING CAN SEPARATE YOU FROM GOD'S LOVE.

God's love is so powerful that NOTHING can come between you and His love for you. His love for you moved His heart and He gave you His best so you could experience victory over the power of sin. Because God demonstrated this kind of love, Paul expresses in this Scripture that there are no limits to God's love: "He who did not spare his own Son, but gave him up for us all—how will he not also, along with him, graciously give us all things?" God's love doesn't stop short. His love continues to give us victory in all areas of our life.

You may go through trouble in life, but God's love is not absent during these times of trouble. You may experience opposition from situations or people, but they cannot stop the power of God's love toward you.

> If you ever doubt the magnitude of God's love,
> take another look at the Cross.

GOD'S LOVE WILL BRING YOU VICTORY.

God's love will bring "overwhelming victory." If you ever doubt the magnitude of God's love, take another look at the Cross. Let it remind you not only of the sacrifice and death of Christ, but also of Christ's victory over death. God's love will bring you the VICTORY.

REFLECT:

- What is God saying to you through this Scripture?

- What has tried to come between you and God's love for you?

- What area are you praying and believing in for victory?

Day 6
Love as Christ Loves You

"A new command I give you: Love one another. As I have loved you, so you must love one another" (John 13:34).

As a Believer in Christ, we carry His name. We represent Jesus, and in turn, there are certain expectations that He requires of us. To love people as Jesus would love is not a suggestion. It is mandatory. Loving people the way Jesus loves is a high standard. In some cases, it can almost be unattainable. But with His help and our willingness there is room for our love to grow.

Reflecting on how Christ loves you can in turn help motivate you to love the people in your life as He would love.

CHRIST LOVES BY ACCEPTING YOU.

Romans 5:17, "Accept one another, then, just as Christ accepted you, in order to bring praise to God."

When we value people, it will come naturally to accept them and do our best to include them. Pay attention to those who may feel rejected or an outsider. Find ways to include and connect them to others, teams, projects or a shared mission. Christ accepted you and adopted you in to His family. When you accept and include others you are loving like Christ. Your acceptance will open the hearts of people to the acceptance of Christ.

CHRIST LOVES BY FORGIVING YOU.

Ephesians 4:32, "Be kind and compassionate to one another, forgiving each other, just as in Christ God forgave you."

Think about how Jesus has forgiven you. When you fall short, make mistakes or display the wrong attitude, Jesus doesn't hold it over your head, or keep reminding you of your wrong or thinks of you differently. He simply forgives. Be personally quick to forgive when someone offends you. Step up your level of love by being quick to forgive before they ask for forgiveness.

CHRIST LOVES BY SACRIFICING FOR YOU.

John 15:13, "Greater love has no one than this: to lay down one's life for one's friends."

Living to serve people is a powerful demonstration of love. Serving people means a life of sacrifice. When you serve people, you become the arms and the hands of Jesus. Your serving is an extension of Jesus and will open people's heart to His love.

CHRIST LOVES BY PRAYING FOR YOU.

Jesus prays for your faith to not fail (Luke 22:32).
Jesus prays that you will be protected from evil (John 17:15).
Jesus intercedes for you every day (Hebrews 7:25).

REFLECT:

- What is God saying to you through this Scripture?

- Where do you feel the love of Christ's prayers for you?

- Write a prayer for your...
    - family.

    - friends.

    - co-workers.

    - the people who do not like you or have mistreated you.

Day 7
Growing Love

"And this is my prayer: that your love may abound more and more in knowledge and depth of insight" (Philippians 1:9).

God desires our love to experience perpetual growth. Growing love is not something that happens naturally. Love is not something that happens magically to us but rather a decision. We choose to love and we must be intentional about our love growing.

HEALTHY LOVE WILL INCREASE NOT DECREASE.

Healthy love shows signs of increase, not decrease. Our love for others can start of well. However, when we are frustrated or aggravated with someone our love can wear thin. We must assess the stamina of our love, especially when an offense has been committed toward us. Healthy love will not decrease and move away from the person who offended, but rather find a way to resolve and forgive. God desires for our love to increase and flourish.

> Healthy love will not decrease and move away
> from the person who offended, but rather find a
> way to resolve and forgive.

LOVE GROWS IN KNOWLEDGE.

The more we know and understand how Jesus loves us, the more our love is able to mature. Discerning how our love should align with God's Word will prompt us to make positive changes to move from superficial love to love that has substance and is meaningful.

The knowledge and discernment that comes from God always brings fresh revelation about ourselves, our relationships and how to address certain situations. Wisdom and discernment will ensure that our response is a love in action that Christ would choose and not one that our flesh would choose. Our action of love can mean well, but if it is not regulated with wisdom and insight, that action of love could be counterintuitive.

Our love will increase and grow as we become great students of the life of Christ, spend time in His Word and listening in His presence. Pray for God's love to flourish in your life and in the life of other Believers around you.

Love in action will grow and mature.

REFLECT:

- What is God saying to you through this Scripture?

- Identify where your action of love can be counterintuitive if not guided by wisdom and insight.

- Ask God to give insight where He desires your love to grow.

Day 8
Love Yourself

"The second is this: 'Love your neighbor as yourself.' There is no commandment greater than these" (Mark 12:31).

If we are unable to have a healthy respect for ourselves we will have a hard time loving and respecting the people in our life. We are tempted with jealousy when we have a very low view or value of who we are. In this state of mind, we may even view people and their accomplishments as threats. Demonstrating God's love is not possible with this kind of feeling. Feeling threatened or jealous are poisonous feelings. And we must remove them so they do not become a detriment to the way that God wants us to love others.

YOUR PERSPECTIVE OF YOU.

When our perspective is healthy, we feel sincerely happy when others experience success or accomplish a great task, just like we want others to celebrate when we have success.

It's ok to recognize where we need to improve. However, do not allow your weaknesses to affect your perspective of your abilities and who God has made you to be.

A key to being able to love yourself is acknowledging that God is your Creator and Designer. He made you. You don't love yourself because you think you are better than everyone. You love yourself because God created you, He loves the way He made you and He paid a great price for you.

GOD DOESN'T MAKE JUNK.

In her autobiography, His Eye Is on the Sparrow, Ethel Waters shares her story: "I was never a child. I never was coddled, or liked, or understood by my family. I never felt I belonged. I was always an outsider.... Nobody brought me up."[4] Ethel Waters's mother was raped at knifepoint. Because the way Ethel was conceived, her mother had a difficult time accepting her as a child. Ethel was tossed around from family member to family member. She was raised in the slums of Philadelphia, Pennsylvania and dropped out of school to support herself by cleaning houses.

But God's amazing grace touched Ethel's heart and her life. She became a very successful singer and actress, and she made history in being the first black woman to appear on radio, to star at the Palace Theater in New York, to introduce 50 songs that became hits, to appear on television, and many other great accomplishments. Ethel had an understanding of God's grace to which she would often make the statement, "I am somebody cause God don't make no junk." Ethel was stating a powerful truth that gave her a healthy perspective of herself.

YOU SEE JESUS IN YOU.

Accepting our personalities and physical bodies is a way of honoring God. There is a healthy balance in accepting everything – even our imperfections. When we see our imperfections, we need to be motivated to make adjustments. We should strive to do better and improve. We also need to remember that our weaknesses and imperfections let us realize that we need Jesus. He died for our sins and He is in our life to bring positive transformation.

There is no need to reject ourselves because of our imperfections. We can remain confident that Jesus is helping us to make progress.

REFLECT:

- What is God saying to you through this Scripture?

- Identify some of the ways in which you need to embrace who you are. How can you love yourself better so that you can love others better?

Day 9
Love Speaks Louder When You Let Go

"Get rid of all bitterness, rage and anger, brawling and slander, along with every form of malice. Be kind and compassionate to one another, forgiving each other, just as in Christ God forgave you" (Ephesians 4:31-32).

Love speaks louder when you don't hold on to an offense. An offense will grow like a contagious sickness. It will not only consume you over time, but also can spread to those who are closest to you. Even worse, an offense that is not taken care of correctly can hinder our prayers, prevent the blessing of God, and delay God's promises for our lives.

A SIGN THAT YOU LOVE.

Christ-Followers bear the fruit of His Spirit. Giving forgiveness and taking care of an offense correctly is a sign that we are fully surrendered to Christ. It's a sign that we LOVE. Learning how to forgive someone before they ask for forgiveness is a sign that the LOVE of God is active in our life. Forgiving doesn't mean that you condone someone's actions. Instead, it means you are choosing to live your life at a higher EQ (emotional intelligence).

> Learning how to forgive someone before they ask for forgiveness is a sign that the LOVE of God is active in our life.

LET IT GO.

Forgiving will allow you to live free from being a victim; it will bring healing to your body, mind and spirit. You will know that you have let the offense go once it's not constantly on your mind and you stop rehearsing the wrong. Letting go of an offense will require us to seek help from the One who knows how to forgive. Charles Spurgeon said, "Let us go to Calvary to learn how we may be forgiven. And then let us linger there to learn how to forgive."

When you forgive and release an offense you will be an example for others to find healing and victory.

REFLECT:

- What is God saying to you through this Scripture?

- Are there any offenses that you need to bring to Christ in prayer? Ask Him for help in forgiving those who have wronged you.

- How does your demonstration of love impact those who are close to you?

Day 10
How We Love Reveals Our Father

"But I tell you, love your enemies and pray for those who persecute you, that you may be children of your Father in heaven..." (Matthew 5:44-45a)

How we treat our enemies will reveal our Father. It is very natural or human of us to be upset with those who do us wrong. But when we choose a different reaction toward the people who are mean and ugly, it truly shows that our Father is living on the inside of us and that we have given Him permission to guide our feelings and actions.

> The amount of love and kindness we display reveals the true measure of the Holy Spirit in our life.

When I gave my own life to Christ, He squeezed the meanness out of me, as He poured His love into me. My experience of Christ's love changed my heart and the way in which I seen the world. For the first time, I felt like I was seeing the people in my life the way God was seeing them. Suddenly, I didn't have any enemies – only people who I needed to love and give kindness.

A NEW HEART AND MIND TO LOVE.

Loving our enemies is not easy. It literally requires a new heart and a new mind from Christ. This is what makes us "children of our Father in heaven." When we make the choice to be kind to our enemies, instead of hating or getting even, we are revealing that God is our Father. When we decide to pray for our enemies instead of degrading them, it reveals that our Father has given us a new heart and a new way of thinking.

REFLECT:

- What is God saying to you through this Scripture?

- How does loving your enemies reveal your Heavenly Father?

- What expression of love can you show to your enemies?

Day 11
Nothing Without Love

"If I have the gift of prophecy and can fathom all mysteries and all knowledge, and if I have a faith that can move mountains, but do not have love, I am nothing"
(1 Corinthians 13:2),

There are a lot of good religious things that we can do. The discipline of prayer, attending church and ministering in spiritual gifts are all wonderful things for our spiritual life. However, the Scripture is clear that, while we may be great in these areas, if we do not place a priority on demonstrating love to others, then we are nothing.

ACTIONS WITHOUT LOVE.

A parent or teacher who gives correction to a child or teen without love can cause rebellion or resentment. A spouse who tries to communicate without love can bring division to a relationship. A friend who critiques without love will leave the other friend wounded and hurt.

If I give all of my money and possession to the poor, but I do it motivated by anything but love, I gain nothing with God (1 Corinthians 13:3). Any act of kindness motivated by pride or a desire to be noticed is a selfish motivation. Our actions of kindness and care must be driven only by love.

> If we contend for the truth, righteousness
> and holiness, but do so without love, we are
> missing the point of the mission of Christ.

If we contend for the truth, righteousness and holiness, but do so without love, we are missing the point of the mission of Christ. If we try to correct, disciple or point out where someone is not measuring up as a Christ-Follower, but do so without love, we are a loud screeching obnoxious noise (1 Corinthians 13:1).

> Love is the only force that is not limited or
> will never die.

LOVE IS EVERYTHING.

Knowledge can be used for good and accomplish many things. Gifts of prophecy and understanding will encourage and give direction. But they have limits and will pass with time. However, love is the only force that does not have limits and will never die. (1 Corinthians 13:8).

Faith, hope and love are powerful principles in God's Kingdom. When faith and hope is exercised amazing things can happen. Incredible breakthroughs are made. Hope can give someone a reason to live. Faith will allow people to experience miracles. I want faith and hope active in my life. But God is telling us over and over again in His Word, that the greatest force that He has created is love (1 Corinthians 13:13).

REFLECT:

- What is God saying to you through this Scripture?

- What are some descriptions of love that stand out to you when you read 1 Corinthians 13?

- What are some ways that you can place a higher priority on demonstrating love to others?

Day 12
Love is the Better Way

"...The only thing that counts is faith expressing itself through love" (Galatians 5:6b).

WE ARE A BETTER VERSION OF OURSELVES WHEN WE LOVE.

To illustrate this principle, let's think about anger. Anger appears to be the opposite of love. Everyone experiences some level of anger. Anger is a justified human emotion. However, we are instructed in the Bible, **"In your anger do not sin: Do not let the sun go down while you are still angry,"** (Ephesians 4:26).

God doesn't expect us to never be angry. He does want us to consider how we express our anger. Is it possible to be angry and yet to still love? We can. We just need to carefully choose the right reaction to our emotion of anger.

Keep this in mind: people are not getting the best out of you when you are doing the opposite of love.

- My anger should motivate me to resolve the situation as quickly as I can, and to not let it linger for days.

- Anger should not lead me to seek revenge or to hurt someone or personally attack them with my words.

- Anger should not be permitted to destroy my relationships.

- I can be angry and still communicate a course of action that brings resolution.

No matter if it's anger, or another emotion or situation, the best version of you is when you act in love.

WE BRING THE BEST OUT OF PEOPLE WHEN WE LOVE.

Someone didn't give up on you. They believed in you. Someone cared enough to help, to correct, to encourage and to instruct you. Someone demonstrated an action of love, and it impacted your life. **The action of love always brings positive results.**

When you love, you bring the best out of people by…

- seeing the good in them that they may not be able to see.

- speaking the right words to help their perspective or change their emotion.

- helping to discover solutions to their problems.

"When love goes up, everything goes up.
Love is always the better way."

REFLECT:

- What is God revealing about Himself through this scripture?

- What action of love will you take today that will bring the best out of people?

Day 13
Love Broke Thru

"For the Son of Man came to seek and to save the lost" (Luke 19:10).

I love Toby Mac's song, **"When Love Broke Thru."** His lyrics resonate with me:

Verse 2,

> "I did all that I could to undo me
> But You loved me enough to pursue me
> Yeah, You drew me out of the shadows
> Made me believe that I mattered, to You, You"

Chorus:

> "When love broke through
> You found me in the darkness
> Wanderin' through the desert
> I was a hopeless fool
> Now I'm hopelessly devoted
> My chains are broken
> And it all began with You
> When love broke through
> And it all began with You
> When love broke through"[5]

LOVE PURSUES.

What is so awesome about God is, He **IS** love. He is the very essence of love. His love looks like pursuing people. Love pursues. Love finds what is lost. Love goes after the broken, and it offers healing. Love makes people feel that they are valuable and that they matter.

Jesus illustrated this **"love pursuit"** with the woman who lost a coin (**Luke 15:8-10**). She has nine more, so what's the big deal? How many coins do you find on the street that people dropped and didn't bother to pick it up? But to this woman, every coin was valuable to her. She would not stop the pursuit until she found the lost coin.

LOVE BREAKS THROUGH.

Every person matters to God. He will not stop His pursuit until they are found, restored and healed. People need breakthroughs. Breakthroughs can be traced back to actions of love.

Think about the breakthroughs you have experienced in your own life. Someone was willing to pursue you and to share Christ with you. Someone loved you enough to pray with you until you experienced a breakthrough. Someone opened their heart and met a need in your life. God pursues because He loves. And He moves the heart of His people to do the same. **When we love, we pursue and love breaks through.**

REFLECT:

- What is God revealing about Himself through this scripture?

- Where can you see God pursuing you throughout your life?

- How can your love be a breakthrough for someone in your life?

Day 14
Love Made Perfect

"And as we live in God, our love grows more perfect. So we will not be afraid on the day of judgment, but we can face him with confidence because we live like Jesus here in this world" (1 John 4:17).

This verse is one major reason why we long to keep our relationship and love for God strong. It is packed with spiritual truth and principles. Reading God's Word, praying, seeking God through fasting, remaining faithful to worship, serving in ministry, giving to God's ministry, and taking inventory of our attitude and behaviors to ensure we are producing the fruit of the Spirit; all of these things are only a few examples of living in God. **Living in God is to not only have a desire to be in God's presence, but to love the things and people He loves.**

> Living in God is to not only have a desire to
> be in God's presence, but to love the things
> and people He loves.

HEAR GOD'S HEARTBEAT OF LOVE.

Here is a first observation from this scripture: we realize that our love can grow into perfection. If you feel like you are not able to love like Christ would love, make an effort to come closer to God. If you sense that you are being tempted to live a selfish life, come closer to the heart of God. The more time we spend with God, the more that we can learn how He loves.

The people in our lives need us to love the way God loves. We cannot afford to let our love be exhausted or limited. This will require us to draw from God's love.

"The closer you draw near to God the more you can hear and feel His heartbeat. God's heart overflows with love. Spend time with Him and you will be a better lover."

REFLECT:

- What is God revealing about Himself through this scripture?

- How does God love differently from us?

- Where may God be asking you to perfect your love?

Day 15
The Love Test

"You have heard that it was said, 'Love your neighbor and hate your enemy.' But I tell you, love your enemies and pray for those who persecute you, that you may be children of your Father in heaven. 46 If you love those who love you, what reward will you get? 48 Be perfect, therefore, as your heavenly Father is perfect" (Matthew 5:43-45a; 46; 48).

One true test of how perfect our love is, is how we treat the people who despise us. Jack Hyles said, **"You will never really love until you love someone who hates you."** It can be very difficult to love someone who has hurt you, whether this hurt has been physical, emotional or even verbal. How we handle the hurt can be a test in and of itself. But how we treat the person who has hurt us is a total different test altogether. This is a test to evaluate the perfection or integrity of our love.

THE TEST OF LOVE.

Rick Warren said, **"God teaches us to love, by putting some unlovely people around us. It takes no character to love people who are lovely and loving to you."** It is really easy to love people who have a sweet attitude or someone who is friendly and outgoing. But what about a person who has a hateful disposition? Someone who is bitter and mean-spirited? God may be placing people in your life for a reason. Consider that your love may need to be perfected. Practicing love in unloving situations will perfect your love. Also, consider that these are the people who God wants to experience His love through you. You may be a key to their breakthrough by your response of love toward them.

HOW TO LOVE YOUR ENEMY.

Dietrich Bonhoeffer, a German pastor who suffered and was killed in Nazi Germany, shared his thoughts on Matthew 5:44, **"is the supreme demand in all of Scripture, to pray for your enemies."** He said, **"By prayer, we go to our enemy's side and we stand with him and plead for him to God."**[6] You and I probably will not be "BFF's" or "besties" with our enemies. But here are two things we can do to show the love of God:

#1. Don't seek revenge. Don't retaliate, hate in return, or talk about them behind their backs. Love speaks louder than hatefulness or revenge.

#2. Pray for them. This is what Jesus is commanding us to do, so our love will be perfect. This is loving like God loves.

THE BONUS FOR THE REWARD (MATTHEW 5:46).

Jesus asked the question. "If you love those who love you, what reward will you get?" To take your love to an even higher level, let's add a #3. Like on a test, you have a "bonus" question. This is the bonus for your reward:

#3. Act of Love. For the one who has hurt you, do something nice in return. Give them a gift card or buy them a gift.

> "God loved us and gave us something we didn't deserve. This is loving like God loves."

Reflect:

- What is God revealing about Himself through this scripture?

- How do you think God may be testing you when it comes to loving others the way He would love?

- Can you identify someone in your life who dislikes you? Have you truly forgiven him or her?

- What is God asking you to do for those who do not like you or have done something to hurt you?

- How do you believe God will reward you as you forgive and/or love others?

Day 16
Love Is Patient

"Therefore, as God's chosen people, holy and dearly loved, clothe yourselves with compassion, kindness, humility, gentleness and patience. Bear with each other and forgive one another if any of you has a grievance against someone. Forgive as the Lord forgave you" (Colossians 3:12-13).

Exercising patience does not come easily for most people. I admit, I can get impatient at times. Long lines, heavy traffic, or experiencing one delay after another while trying to finish a project all test my patience.

There is a strong connection in showing love to the people around us who need our patience. For relationships to grow, we must learn how to "bear" one another. Learn how to tolerate each other's differences and shortcomings. This is not easy. But if we think about how God is patient with us, then maybe we will be in a better mindset to be patient with others.

2 Peter 3:9, "The Lord isn't really being slow about his promise, as some people think. No, he is being patient for your sake. He does not want anyone to be destroyed but wants everyone to repent."

God displays His love for us by being patient with us when we have failed, made mistakes and didn't display the right attitude. He desires for us to show others the same kind of love.

LOVE BY GIVING PATIENCE WHEN...

- you have to spend extra time helping your children with homework or a school project. (And they are showing visible signs that they are not motivated to learn.)

- a person is having a bad day and they are rude to you.

- someone is aggravating you because of their quirkiness, loud mouth, silence or annoying habits.

- you are going through trials, feeling misunderstood, or being persecuted.

We need the Holy Spirit to help us produce patience.

May we depend on the Holy Spirit who is the one that produces true LOVE in our life (Galatians 5:22). Patience is the fruit He produces in our life. As we keep the sensitivity of the Holy Spirit in our hearts, **"love suffers long and is kind"** (1 Corinthians 13:4), this will be our attitude, behavior and our act of love.

REFLECT:

- What is God revealing about Himself through this scripture?

- Where is God asking you to exercise patience?

Day 17
Love Gives

"You must each decide in your heart how much to give. And don't give reluctantly or in response to pressure. "For God loves a person who gives cheerfully" (2 Corinthians 9:7).

Everything that we have is a result of our Heavenly Father giving to us. God has given us health, time, skills, abilities, knowledge, jobs, finances, wealth, resources, a network of connections, and friendships. This is by far not an exhaustive list. If you pause for a moment, your mind will be flooded with things that God has given to you.

God desires for us to be good stewards of everything He has given to us. We are more like God when we give. And when we are "givers," we are showing God's love. By giving we keep selfishness and self-centeredness out of our life. "Some people are always greedy for more, but the godly love to give! (Proverbs 21:26)

YOUR LOVE INSPIRES YOU TO GIVE.

Giving cheerfully brings joy to God's heart. When you love to give, you bring a smile to God's face.

2 Corinthians 9:7

Giving is an act of worship. "God you have given me everything. Here is a small expression of my gratefulness and attitude toward You."

Psalm 116:12, "What shall I return to the LORD for all his goodness to me?"

1 Chronicles 16:29,"Give to the LORD the glory he deserves! Bring your offering and come into his presence. Worship the LORD in all his holy splendor."

Giving demonstrates God's Salvation God gives sacrificially, and your own giving is a demonstration of God's Salvation to the people who you are influencing. You impact people's lives through your giving.

John 3:16, "For God so loved the world that he gave his one and only Son, that whoever believes in him shall not perish but have eternal life."

Giving reveals God's heart. You are a reflection of God. Someone said, "You are the only Jesus that most people will see." We are inspired to give because our Heavenly Father has blessed us. **Giving allows people to see the heart of God. When people see your generosity, it inspires them to greatness.** Stinginess never inspires.

James 1:17, "Every good and perfect gift is from above, coming down from the Father of the heavenly lights, who does not change like shifting shadows."

WHAT DO WE GIVE?

We give…

- our time to volunteer.

- love to the people in our lives.

- money to support needs, worship God, help ministry efforts, spread the gospel, support God's Kingdom.

- skills to accomplish God's mission and to make things better.

- our words to comfort, to affirm and to encourage.

- our companionship to those who are lonely and need a friend.

THE BLESSING THAT COMES WITH GIVING.

God will bless you for your love of giving.

- Proverbs 22:9 "The generous will themselves be blessed, for they share their food with the poor."

- Proverbs 28:27, "Those who give to the poor will lack nothing, but those who close their eyes to them receive many curses."

- Malachi 3:9-11 - God will open the heavens and protect your investments as a result of your giving.

> "You bring glory to God when your love gives. Your love speaks louder when you give."

REFLECT:

- What is God revealing about Himself through this scripture?

- Where is God asking you to give as a demonstration of love?

- How will giving be a sacrifice for you?

Day 18
Sometimes Love Is What You Don't Say

"Kind words bring life, but cruel words crush your spirit" (Proverbs 15:4).

We should always be truthful, but never at the cost of being rude or inconsiderate of other people's feelings. Rudeness is selfish and prideful. Being overly critical and blunt will wound the soul and may even crush someone's spirit.

One characteristic of love is expressing words. The words we choose will either encourage or discourage. Build up or teardown. Heal or crush.

Charlotte Mortimer shared her own experience in a class project about writing words of love. "The teacher in our adult-education creative-writing class told us to write 'I love you' in 25 words or less, without using the words 'I love you.' She gave us 15 minutes. A woman in the class spent about ten minutes looking at the ceiling and wriggling in her seat. The last five minutes she wrote frantically, and later read us the results:

'Why, I've seen lots worse hairdos than that, honey.'

'These cookies are hardly burned at all.'

'Cuddle up-I'll get your feet warm.'"[7]

Please allow me to be honest. After reading this list, I believe my wife, Bonnie could rewrite several sentences that I have rudely stated to her in 25 years of marriage. I'm reminded that "love is not rude" (1 Corinthians 13:5). However, I have seen the error of my ways. I realize that love can be expressed by choosing the right words.

LOVE SPEAKS LOUDER, BECAUSE LOVE SPEAKS LIFE.

Choosing to be blunt may come more naturally to some than to others. This is where we rely on the new life and the new creation that God places within us when we receive Jesus Christ. The new nature has come and the old nature has gone (2 Corinthians 5:17). Yes, it does take effort. We pause before we speak. We demonstrate love by articulating in a way that is kind, thoughtful and encouraging. The Bible tells us we have the ability to speak life. **"The tongue has the power of life and death, and those who love it will eat its fruit"** (Proverbs 18:21).

> People who love are "life-givers." Love speaks louder, because love speaks life. Your kind words are actions of love.

REFLECT:

- What is God revealing about Himself through this scripture?

- Where or when do you need to exercise silence as a demonstration of love?

- Before responding, try a 10 second pause, evaluating whether the words you are choosing will be life-giving or add hurt or discouragement.

Day 19
Give Love and Never Run Out

"That's the ultimate test of how you have lived your life. The trouble with love is that you can't buy it ... The only way to get love is to be lovable ... The more you give love away, the more you get." These are the words from the famous Warren Buffet.

Warren Buffet claims to be agnostic but chooses to live out a Biblical principle of giving. This principle works because God created it and it works in every area of our life. **"Give, and it will be given to you. A good measure, pressed down, shaken together and running over, will be poured into your lap. For with the measure you use, it will be measured to you"** (Luke 6:38). When we give our time, talent or treasure to others, God gives back to us in return.

God is a personal and a relational God. His desire for us is to give love in the form of giving, care, friendship, words of affirmation, time, prayer and honor. **"Don't just pretend to love others. Really love them. Hate what is wrong. Hold tightly to what is good. Love each other with genuine affection and take delight in honoring each other"** (Romans 12:9-10 NLT).

When we make giving love to others the priority of our lives, we not only honor God's desire for our lives; God will bring blessings in to our lives. Blessing others with love will ensure a life of blessings.

THE ONLY WAY TO RECEIVE IS TO FIRST GIVE.
Remember the story of Job? Job was going through one of the most devastating times in his life. Job's breakthrough didn't come when he

prayed for himself. **Instead, his breakthrough came when he took the time to pray for his friends. "After Job had prayed for his friends, the Lord restored his fortunes and gave him twice as much as he had before"** (Job 42:10 NIV).

When our eyes are only on ourselves and our only concern is what we need, we will continue to be in a state of need and lack. God has blessed us with an amazing relational principle. The more we give toward the needs of others, the more we will find our own needs being met.

"A person who freely gives love away will find no shortage of being loved in return."

REFLECT:

- What is God revealing about Himself through this scripture?

- What breakthroughs do you need in your own life?

- Do you see a need in someone's life around you?

- Where might God be leading you to give an action of love to others?

Day 20
Love Appreciates

"Now concerning brotherly love you have no need for anyone to write to you, for you yourselves have been taught by God to love one another" (1 Thessalonians 4:9).

You give love when you show appreciation to the people in your life. The word appreciation means something that is gaining or increasing in value. A house can either appreciate, increasing in value or depreciate, decreasing in value. Depending on how something is cared for, will determine on how valuable it becomes to you.

When you appreciate your spouse, children, friends, family and the people God has placed in your life, they will begin to increase in value. Failing to give appreciation to the people in your life will eventually lose value in your eyes. We value what we appreciate.

EVERYONE HAS VALUE.
When we take people for granted we do not give proper appreciation. This, in turn, causes us to miss the gift of God in them. Everyone has value. God is at work and has placed treasure inside them. Our love of appreciation brings out the treasure in their lives and we will be blessed by their gifts.

God desires for us to be people who raise the value of others. Everyone needs affirmation and encouragement. From my observation, I believe there is a shortage of this kind of appreciation. We must not be afraid or too prideful to give a compliment and tell someone that they are appreciated. This kind of love raises people's value. Not only will you please God by blessing them with your encouragement, they will truly have a deeper value in your heart as well.

"Love appreciates. Your love raises the
value of others."

REFLECT:

- What is God revealing about Himself through this scripture?

- Can you identify someone in your own life who needs to feel valued? Can you demonstrate an action of love?

- Who in your life do you need to show extra appreciation and honor?

- Take a moment to send an encouraging text, write a card or give an appreciation gift.

Day 21
Revival of Love

"Finally, be all of one mind, be loving toward one another, be gracious, and be kind. Do not repay evil for evil, or curse for curse, but on the contrary, bless, knowing that to this you are called, so that you may receive a blessing. For 'He who would love life and see good days, let him keep his tongue from evil, and his lips from speaking deceit" (1 Peter 3:8-10).

There are many great people in the world. I have been deeply blessed to have met some of the most caring, loving people over the years - people who have prayed for me when I was going through struggles. Some have given their support when others would not; others gave out of appreciation.

I have also met some really mean people who probably were acting out of their own hurt and insecurities – or maybe they just didn't have a real change of heart and perspective on life. We see in the news evil acts of hatred, racism, injustices, bullying, political division and many other acts that are the opposite of love.

THE POWER OF LOVE.

The only thing that will bring healing and attract people to Christ's Salvation is when we demonstrate His love. Jesus said our love will stand out to the people around. **John 13:35**, "Your love for one another will prove to the world that you are my disciples."

This is a common theme throughout God's Word that instructs us to bless others. I really do love this because it gives us purpose. We are to be people who bless. The scripture in **1 Peter 3:8-10** declares that

59

this is our calling – a calling to bless, a calling to love. A calling from God means that we are empowered by His Spirit to love.

AWAKENED LOVE.

A revival of love means that God's love can be awakened in us to a new level. We can see people as God sees people. The Holy Spirit will give us creativity and words of knowledge on how to show God's love to the people around us. When God's love is revived within us, we begin to be sensitive to people's needs around us.

> "Our acts of love will draw people to Christ more than our opinions or voicing our differences."

REFLECT:

- What is God revealing about Himself through this scripture?

- What breakthroughs do you need in your own life?

- Do you see a need in someone's life around you?

- Where might God be leading to giving an action of love to others?

Love in Action

Love is not experienced until it is expressed. Love is not just a feeling – instead, it is demonstrated with action. Love must be intentional. You can make an action of love intentional by scheduling an action of love in your daily schedule. Prepare by taking the necessary resources and items with you on a daily basis. With strong conviction, I believe our love in action should always be done in the name of Jesus Christ. I believe that we should let the person know that we are giving or expressing love in action because of the love of Christ. We should never take credit for something He has started in our life. Our acts of love should always lead people back to Jesus.

The following are several suggestions to help you put love in to action.

- Make a connection with a widow in your neighborhood or church and volunteer to help with yard or a house repair.
- Pay for someone's coffee or lunch behind you in the
- drive-thru.
- Offer to babysit for free.
- Send a card of encouragement to someone.
- Bake cookies for your neighbor, postman or delivery person.
- Leave an extravagant tip for your server at a restaurant.
- Give financially to someone you know who is struggling.
- Take breakfast, bagels or lunch to the police or fire department.
- Donate diapers, wipes and your time to the pregnancy center.
- Take breakfast or lunch to teachers at a local daycare.
- Purchase $10, $20 or more gift cards from grocery store and be ready to give to someone random in the community.

- Allow God to lead you to someone as He prompts your heart.
- Take donuts or bagels to the janitors and office staff at local school.
- Take coins and detergent to a local laundry mat and give away.
- Do a chore that is on your spouse's list.
- Leave a note of encouragement for your spouse.
- Wash and vacuum a friend's car.
- Take someone to lunch who may be lonely or going through a hard time.
- Volunteer your time to a local soup kitchen or church.
- Offer a ride to someone who does not have a car.
- Get your children involved in demonstrating love. Help them show love and appreciation by giving things to their teachers at school, bus drivers, coaches, teachers at church and also to their friends.
- Do you know someone who recently lost a loved one? Give a gift, take them to lunch, take some time for them.
- Organize a food drive for your local food pantry.
- Pay the bill for a family dining in at the table next to you at a restaurant.
- Help families that have adopted children or are involved in foster care in your church or community.

"And let us consider how we may spur one another on toward love and good deeds" (Hebrews 10:24).

Love Scriptures

"For God so loved the world that he gave his one and only Son, that whoever believes in him shall not perish but have eternal life." **John 3:16**

"Greater love has no one than this: to lay down one's life for one's friends." **John 15:13**

"So now I am giving you a new commandment: Love each other. Just as I have loved you, you should love each other. Your love for one another will prove to the world that you are my disciples." **John 13:34-35**

"There is no fear in love. But perfect love drives out fear, because fear has to do with punishment. The one who fears is not made perfect in love. We love because He first loved us." **1 John 4:18-19**

"Above all, love each other deeply, because love covers over a multitude of sins." **1 Peter 4:8**

"But God demonstrates his own love for us in this: While we were still sinners, Christ died for us." **Rom. 5:8**

"But you, O Lord, are a compassionate and gracious God, slow to anger, abounding in love and faithfulness." **Psalm 86:15**

"Let all that you do be done in love." **1 Corinthians 16:14**

"So now faith, hope, and love abide, these three; but the greatest of these is love." **1 Corinthians 13:13**

"Dear friends, let us love one another, for love comes from God. Everyone who loves has been born of God and knows God. Whoever does not love does not know God, because God is love." **1 John 4:7-8**

"If you love me, you will obey what I command." **John 14:15**

"Above all, be loving. This ties everything together perfectly." **Colossians 3:14**

"Hate stirs up trouble, but love forgives all offenses." **Proverbs 10:12**

"Love must be sincere. Hate what is evil; cling to what is good. Be devoted to one another in brotherly love. Honor one another above yourselves." **Romans 12:9-10**

"Give thanks to the Lord, for he is good; his love endures forever." **1 Chronicles 16:34**

"A friend loves at all times, and a brother is born for a time of adversity." **Proverbs 17:17**

"The Lord your God is with you, he is mighty to save. He will take great delight in you, he will quiet you with his love, he will rejoice over you with singing." **Zephaniah 3:17**

"He has shown you, O man, what is good. And what does the Lord require of you? To act justly and to love mercy and to walk humbly with your God." **Micah 6:8**

"Be completely humble and gentle; be patient, bearing with one another in love." **Ephesians 4:2**

"For Christ's love compels us, because we are convinced that one died for all, and therefore all died." **2 Corinthians 5:14**

"But love your enemies, do good to them, and lend to them without expecting to get anything back. Then your reward will be great..." **Luke 6:35**

"Husbands, love your wives, as Christ loved the church and gave himself up for her." **Ephesians 5:25**

"But you are a forgiving God, gracious and compassionate, slow to anger and abounding in love..." **Nehemiah 9:17**

"Let them give thanks to the Lord for his unfailing love and his wonderful deeds for men, for he satisfies the thirsty and fills the hungry with good things." **Psalm 107:8-9**

"For you have been called to live in freedom, my brothers and sisters. But don't use your freedom to satisfy your sinful nature. Instead, use your freedom to serve one another in love. For the whole law can be summed up in this one command: 'Love your neighbor as yourself.'" **Galatians 5:13-14**

"But the fruit of the Spirit is love, joy, peace, patience, kindness, goodness, faithfulness, gentleness and self-control." **Galatians 5:22-23**

"Owe no one anything, except to love each other, for the one who loves another has fulfilled the law." **Romans 13:8**

"Your love, O Lord, reaches to the heavens, your faithfulness to the skies. Your righteousness is like the mighty mountains, your justice like the great deep." **Psalm 36:5-6**

"Live a life of love, just as Christ loved us and gave himself up for us as a fragrant offering and sacrifice to God." **Ephesians 5:2**

"Anyone who claims to be in the light but hates his brother is still in the darkness. Whoever loves his brother lives in the light, and there is nothing in him to make him stumble." **1 John 2:9-10**

"How great is the love the Father has lavished on us, that we should be called children of God!" **1 John 3:1**

"This is how we know what love is: Jesus Christ laid down his life for us. And we ought to lay down our lives for our brothers. If anyone has material possessions and sees his brother in need but has no pity on him, how can the love of God be in him? Dear children, let us not love with words or tongue but with actions and in truth."
1 John 3:16-18

"This is how God showed his love among us: He sent his one and only Son into the world that we might live through him. This is love: not that we loved God, but that he loved us and sent his Son as an atoning sacrifice for our sins. Dear friends, since God so loved us, we also ought to love one another." **1 John 4:9-11**

"His banner over me is love." **Song of Songs 2:4**

"The commandments…are summed up in the one command, 'Love your neighbor as you love yourself.' If you love others, you will

never do them wrong, to love, then, is to obey the whole
Law." **Romans 13:9-10**

"Place me like a seal over your heart, like a seal on your arm; for love
is as strong as death...Many waters cannot quench love; rivers cannot
wash it away." **Song of Songs 8:6-7**

"I have been crucified with Christ and I no longer live, but Christ
lives in me. The life I live in the body, I live by faith in the Son of
God, who loved me and gave himself for me." **Galatians 2:20**

"I will declare that your love stands firm forever, that you established
your faithfulness in heaven itself." **Psalm 89:2**

"The earth is filled with your love, O Lord..." **Psalm 119:64**

"You were cleansed from your sins when you obeyed the truth, so
now you must show sincere love to each other as brothers and
sisters. Love each other deeply with all your heart." **1 Peter 1:22**

"Jesus replied: 'Love the Lord your God with all your heart and with
all your soul and with all your mind.' This is the first and greatest
commandment. And the second is like it: 'Love your neighbor as
yourself.'" **Matthew 22:37-39**

"In all these things, we are more than conquerors through him who
loved us. For I am convinced that neither death or life, neither
angels nor demons, neither the present nor the future, nor any
powers, neither height nor depth, nor anything else in all creation,
will be able to separate us from the love of God that is in Christ Jesus
our Lord." **Romans 8:37-39**

"For God did not give us a spirit of timidity, but a spirit of power, of love, and of self-discipline." **1 Timothy 1:7**

"Show proper respect to everyone: Love the brotherhood of believers, fear God, honor the king." **1 Peter 2:17**

"But be very careful…to love the Lord your God, to walk in all his ways, to obey his commands, to hold fast to him and to serve him with all your heart and all your soul." **Joshua 22:5**

"'Though the mountains be shaken and the hills be removed, yet my unfailing love for you will not be shaken nor my covenant of peace be removed,' says the Lord, who has compassion on you."
Isaiah 54:10

"Let love and faithfulness never leave you; bind them around your neck, write them on the tablet of your heart. Then you will win favor and a good name in the sight of God and man." **Proverbs 3:3-4**

"May the Lord make your love increase and overflow for each other…" **1Thess. 3:12**

"Love is patient, love is kind. It does not envy, it does not boast, it is not proud. It is not rude, it is not self-seeking, it is not easily angered, it keeps no record of wrongs. Love does not delight in evil but rejoices with the truth. It always protects, always trusts, always hopes, always perseveres. Love never fails…" **1 Corinthians 13:4-7**

"Because your love is better than life, my lips will glorify you."
Psalm 63:3

ABOUT THE AUTHOR

David Shannon Wooten is the lead pastor at Newspring Church in Springboro, Ohio. Shannon's passion is to encourage people in their journey of faith in Christ. He has dedicated over 25 years teaching Biblical principles that inspire and equip people with practical application. Shannon has mentored individuals and has coached church leaders to help reach their full-potential. He has helped revitalized churches and has successfully led the merger of two churches.

Shannon, his wife Bonnie and their children Shantelle, Shalene and Ross reside in the Cincinnati/Dayton Ohio area.

You can connect with Shannon by following his blog at davidshannonwooten.com and on social media. You can also listen to messages or join a live service online at newspringlive.com.

NOTES

[1] The American Heritage® Dictionary of the English Language, Fifth Edition copyright ©2018 by Houghton Mifflin Harcourt Publishing Company. All rights reserved.

[2] Blaise Pascal, Pensees, (New York; Penguin Books, 1966) 75.

[3] Ravi Zacharias, The Grand Weaver: How God Shapes Us Through the Events of Our Lives, (Zondervan, 2007) 49.

[4] Ethel Waters, His Eye is on the Sparrow: An Autobiography (Da Capo Press, 1992).

[5] TobyMac - Official Music Video for "Love Broke Thru" (C) 2017 ForeFront Records - www.youtube.com/watch?v=44l9PRI4c2M

[6] Dietrich Bonhoeffer, The Cost of Discipleship, (New York, Macmillan, 1959).

[7] Charlotte Mortimer, in February 1990 *Reader's Digest*.

www.ingramcontent.com/pod-product-compliance
Lightning Source LLC
Chambersburg PA
CBHW060655030426
42337CB00017B/2630